In the War

School Life

Peter Hicks

WAYLAND

First published in 2008 by Wayland

Copyright © Wayland 2008

Wayland
338 Euston Road
London NW1 3BH

Wayland Australia
Level 17/207 Kent Street
Sydney, NSW 2000

Editor: Camilla Lloyd
Designer: Phipps Design
Picture researcher: Shelley Noronha

Acknowledgments:
Inside Stories from 'Interview with the author': p.8, p.11, p.12, p.15, p.18, p.26; p.4 from *How We Lived Then* by Norman Longmate (Hutchinson, 1971) p.49; p.7 from *Goodnight Children Everywhere: Memories of Evacuation in WWII* Ed. Pam Schweitzer (Age Exchange Theatre Trust, 1990) p.69, p.20 from *Goodnight Children Everywhere* by Pam Schweitzer p.207, p.23 from *Goodnight Children Everywhere* by Pam Schweitzer p.150, p.24 from *Goodnight Children Everywhere* by Pam Schweitzer p.150, p.29 from *Goodnight Children Everywhere* by Pam Schweitzer p.43; p.16 from *Children of War* by Susan Goodman (John Murray, 2005).

Picture Acknowledgments: The author and publisher would like to thank the following for their pictures to be reproduced in this publication: Cover photographs: Wayland Picture Library (both);
© Bettman/Corbis: 15, 26, © Corbis: 13, © Hulton-Deutsch Collection/Corbis: 6, 10, 16, 17, 20, 23, 25; Roger Viollet/Topfoto: 18, Topfoto: 8, 14, 19, 21, 22, 27, 28; Wayland Picture Library: 1, 4, 5, 7, 9, 11, 12., 24, 29.

British Library Cataloguing in Publication Data:
Hicks, Peter, 1952-
    School life. - (In the war)
    1. Schools - Great Britain - History - 20th century -
    Juvenile literature 2. World War, 1939-1945 - Children -
    Great Britain - Juvenile literature 3. World War, 1939-1945
    - Social aspects - Great Britain - Juvenile literature
    I. Title
    370.9'41'09044

ISBN: 978 0 7502 5353 6

Printed in China

Wayland is a division of Hachette Children's Books, an Hachette Livre UK company

Contents

Beginnings

During the summer of 1939, a serious international crisis came about over Poland. The leader of Nazi Germany, Adolf Hitler was demanding the Polish port of Danzig on the Baltic Sea. Britain, and her ally France, who had promised to protect the Poles from attack, were prepared to declare war on Germany if they invaded Poland. By the end of August 1939, war looked highly likely and the British government took steps to protect its **civilian** population from attack.

The big fear in the 1930s was that air attacks or raids from bomber aircraft would cause great destruction to the big cities.

Evacuee children boarding a train. They had no idea where they were going.

It would be essential to move school-age children out of the cities and into the safety of the countryside. The order for this **evacuation** was given on 30 August 1939 and during the following few days over 1.5 million children were transported by hundreds of trains to safe destinations all over the country.

Parents decided whether their children should be evacuated. If they agreed, they were to send them to school with spare clothes, toothbrush, comb and food for the day. They walked or got the bus to the nearest station where they were sent to unknown destinations. When the children arrived at safe towns and villages they were **billeted** with other families.

On 1 September, Nazi Germany unleashed its planes and tanks on Poland. Britain and France told Germany to withdraw or face war. Hitler ignored this warning, so on the 3 September 1939, Britain and France declared war on Germany.

What was to happen to the education of the evacuee children?

Newpaper headline, Thursday, 31 August 1939. The 'decision' to evacuate was a big shock for many people.

Think about
How do you think you would feel if you were sent away without knowing where you were going?

Problems

Once the children were safely billeted away from the cities and had settled in with their 'new families', thought was given to their schooling. In many places it was hit and miss. Where enough teachers had accompanied the children makeshift lessons were provided. School accommodation proved to be a problem. One school from Croydon was able to take over a village hall for weekday mornings and spent afternoons on nature rambles or playing football on the village 'rec' (recreation ground). Schools took over public houses, churches, chapels and cricket pavilions!

Some children had no schooling at all. One evacuee, at an unfriendly home in Kent, remembers being ordered out with her brother at 8.30 every morning in all weather and told to 'Go and play.' After a cold snack for lunch the order was repeated and they were not allowed back inside until 4.30 in the afternoon.

These boys from Malvern school found themselves staying at Blenheim Palace, home to the Duke of Marlborough!

Think about
If you were very unhappy in your new home, like the girl in Kent, what would you do?

As expected lots of children were very homesick and hated being parted from their parents. It is not surprising that when the bombs failed to fall on the cities – this period of the conflict was called the 'Phoney War' when nothing really happened – many parents brought their children home. By January 1940, nearly half of all evacuated children were back in their own homes and by the spring, the majority had returned.

When they came back to the cities they found the school system had broken down. Many schools were closed and taken over for Civil Defence (protection from air-raids). Schools remained shut because they did not have air-raid shelters. In some areas, children ran around with nothing to do but get into trouble.

INSIDE STORY:

'Our village school had a playground but also a large playing field behind. I thought it was wonderful. I had never seen a grass playground in London. There was so much room for everybody!'

These children from a state school in South London, found that their new school in Wales was a village hall.

Blitz!

When most of the evacuees returned in early 1940, there were few educational facilities for them. 'Home schools' were a short-term solution. A room in a private house could be rented for about 2s 6d (12 ½p) a week and groups of up to 12 children were taught in them. This was first tried by the authorities in Sheffield, but was then adopted by most cities. Basic reading and writing were taught for an hour and a half a day with games at the local park and visits to the local library.

The Prime Minister, Winston Churchill, inspects bomb damage in the port of Bristol. The area of the port and aircraft factories were obvious targets.

INSIDE STORY:

'On our first evacuation we were sent to Balcombe in Sussex, but we were all back by Christmas. During the summer of 1940, half the school was sent much further away, to Devon, not far from Exeter.'

By June 1940, the situation changed again when the German army overran the Low Countries and France. All the children in the southeast, northeast and on the east coast of Britain were seen to be under threat from a possible German invasion so nearly 215,000 were sent inland away from the coasts. Pressure was again on the schools receiving evacuees. Just as local authorities in the cities were getting on top of the school problem the German Air Force began to drop bombs in September 1940, this was called the **Blitz**. The Blitz damaged or destroyed many schools and children's education suffered greatly.

A teacher leads out his class, all wearing gas masks, in Woolwich, southeast London. This school's windows have been damaged by bombs. There is a blast wall in front of the lower windows.

On top of this, school teachers did not stay in their jobs for long. Twenty thousand male teachers were called up to the armed forces so married women were encouraged to return to teaching. Retired or physically unfit males were also encouraged to teach and many had no teaching experience. This led to problems in the classrooms and many classes were told off for being unpatriotic because of their poor behaviour. However, the increase of women teachers was thought to have a good effect on the pupils, especially in all-boys schools.

Think about
Despite the bombs falling a lot of children stayed in the cities with their families. Why do you think this was?

Lessons

The shortage of school buildings created major problems for head teachers trying to provide a basic standard of education. In the **reception areas**, evacuated schools from the cities had to share buildings with the local schools. This brought about a **shift system**. Sometimes the evacuated schools used the school from 1.00 to 4.30 in the afternoon or on alternate days, leaving the other times for the local schools. Mixed classes of different ages were common. Overall, children were spending much less time in school because of the war.

Equipment was in short supply. Exercise books and pencils were sometimes chopped in half and shared. Desperate teachers often drove back to their city schools to collect basic equipment.

What happened to lessons? The **curriculum** had to change due to the war. Some schools lost their sports facilities when the army took over their playing fields. Table tennis replaced traditional team games and many schools taught First Aid instead. Bandages and **splints** were thought to be more useful now that bombs were falling.

These school children in Hackney, London, were taught by the police to recognize weapons and unexploded bombs that might be found in the street.

Think about
What would you and you parents think if your school only provided three hours of lessons a day?

Music and art lessons became more **patriotic** to raise national spirit. Songs such as, 'There'll always be an England', were sung at assemblies. After 1941, drawings of Winston Churchill, Joseph Stalin and Franklin D. Roosevelt (the **Allied** leaders) were encouraged in art lessons. In girls' schools, laundry lessons stressed the importance of saving soap and hot water, as these were especially precious in wartime. Food technology lessons (then called domestic science) mostly disappeared – rationed food was far too precious to waste on cooking lessons – although many pupils learned about vitamins and the balanced diet. When domestic science did take place, recipes were based on vegetables, which were not rationed.

INSIDE STORY:

'It was great – we only did morning school because we shared with the Peckham children from London. We knitted little squares that were made into blankets for them. They had the afternoon slot. Afternoons were free time for us!'

During good weather in the countryside, some teachers taught lessons in the open air!

Air-raid precautions!

Between 1940 and 1941, German planes heavily bombed British towns and cites. The bombings were known as air-raids. Throughout the summer of 1940, the local authorities worked hard to give schools protection from air-raids. **Slit trenches** were the most basic. They were dug into the earth, strengthened with sandbags or timber and were V-shaped or zig-zagged to give protection from the blast. Children caught outside could quickly run into them.

Stronger shelters were needed for large numbers of children. Covered trench shelters protected many schools. Deep trenches were dug into the playground and then covered with concrete or steel frames to protect the sides and roof. Earth from the trenches provided overhead protection.

INSIDE STORY:

'We had a lovely long corridor that we loved running and sliding down when the teachers weren't looking. But then they built some blast walls halfway along them, and our sliding days were over!'

Steel air-raid called Anderson shelters, were delivered to houses in London and assembled in the back garden.

There was electrical lighting or oil lamps were used if there was a power cut. The trenches were entered by a flight of stairs protected by a **blast wall** and a **manhole** was the emergency exit. Other shelters were semi-sunken with the same concrete frames covered by soil and turf.

The shelters had wooden seats on each side and there were usually chemical toilet facilities too. A curtain or flimsy door that hid very little separated the toilets from the main part of the shelter. During an air-raid drill or practice, children ran to the shelter, filed in and sat down, boys on the left and girls on the right. A register was taken and the children put on their gas masks and sat quietly. Many children did not like them because the masks smelt strongly of rubber and made them feel smothered, especially when the Perspex screen steamed up.

Think about

How do you think children felt when they saw air-raid shelters being built in their playgrounds in 1940?

Children await anxiously in a slit trench and search the sky for enemy planes.

In the shelters

As a result of air-raid alerts and raids during 1940-44, many children spent a great deal of time in the shelters. A practice drill usually began with a teacher banging a gong or ringing a bell, but a real air-raid alert started with street sirens going off with a rising and falling sound. Everybody was expected to take cover. When enemy planes were close, electronic 'pips' would sound and by then you had to be in the shelter. If there was no warning and enemy planes appeared suddenly, children took cover under their desks!

A teacher, who was also an air-raid warden, takes the class register in a shelter.

Children sat upright in the shelter, so that teachers could walk through the middle. The children breathed in the damp smells of the unprotected concrete walls. Other children remember the smell of disinfectant from the toilets. No matter what time of year, the underground shelters were always bitterly cold.

Head teachers kept a record of the time spent in the shelters. Many logbooks have comments like: 'the school was in the trenches from 1.45 to 5.45 pm.' What did children do while there were enemy planes in the sky?

Think about
How would you cope with being told to sit still on a bench, in a smelly, cold shelter for three to four hours?

Posion gas was always feared, but it was never actually used in the war. These children in Windsor were well-prepared!

Teachers organized chanting of times tables, pounds, shillings and pence tables and singing. Quizzes were popular and for long alerts children contributed sweets to the 'chocolate monitor', which meant that someone was put in charge of sharing out the sweets.

Night raids and alerts also affected children. With sirens and explosions, many pupils and teachers were very tired. After heavy raids, schools often started later so everyone could catch up on their sleep.

INSIDE STORY:

'Our shelters were dug into the hill at the back of the school. Being chalk, they were quite dry, we didn't mind them. There were two or three raids a week and we quite enjoyed getting out of the classroom. We paid 2d to the chocolate monitor but I don't remember ever getting any!'

Exams and universities

Some children welcomed air-raids as a diversion from school but for those taking examinations during the war, wailing sirens and exploding bombs were the last thing they wanted!

The children look relaxed reading their comics and magazines, even though there was an air-raid taking place.

INSIDE STORY:

'*While we were doing our summer exams we could hear the drone of planes going over for D-Day...It was hard to keep our minds on what we were doing...*'

Some schools actually set up their exams in air-raid shelters in case there was a raid and not surprisingly children became very nervous when the bombs started falling. Many pupils remember being worried about the quality of their handwriting because of nerves and whether the examiner would be able to read it. In fact, the examination boards were very understanding of those affected by raids and asked for teacher's reports concerning their likely grades. They even interviewed each pupil if a particularly bad raid happened during an exam.

You needed to be very tough at this difficult time. One boy, sitting the equivalent of his GCSE's in 1944 was disturbed 13 times by raid alerts, but had to concentrate and carry on. Another girl in south London, doing the equivalent of her 'A'- Levels remembers writing her exam flat on her stomach in the school air-raid shelter!

Think about
Why do you think examinations were still held even though there was a war on?

Universities carried on during the war although many were evacuated to safe areas. Most male students were called up into the armed forces although there were exceptions. Male medical, dentistry, science and engineering students could finish their courses but had to go into the armed forces or 'essential' war work on graduation. The majority of students were therefore female.

Many universities and schools were very old, with ancient timber and libraries so fire was a constant threat during the war. All students had to look out for fires and become experts with a **stirrup pump** in order to put them out!

Here a group of boys are being taught to use a stirrup pump to put out fires.

Help the war effort!

One of the big problems facing Britain during the war was the severe shortage of raw materials. As an island, Britain had to import large amounts of industrial materials and Germany knew this. During the **Battle of the Atlantic** (1939-45), hundreds of ships carrying essential supplies were sunk by German U-Boats. What could be done? The government really encouraged **salvage** or recycling campaigns. Everything from saucepans to rubber tyres could be re-used to help the war effort.

Schools were targeted for the salvage campaign. Speakers from the Ministry of Information visited schools explaining how and what to recycle and of course, the government tapped in on young people's enthusiasm and energy. It was also a clever way of getting children to 'do their bit' and feel they were helping with the war.

Schools used lots of paper and many organized a weekly 'Paper Drive'. Pupils brought in waste paper and it was weighed and sold to a paper merchant.

The playing fields of this school were made into vegetable gardens that were looked after by the pupils.

INSIDE STORY:

'We only went to school in the mornings so in the afternoon we came back to the school allotment and tended to the vegetables. 'Dig for Victory!' was taken quite seriously in my school.'

What would you
have liked to salvage?
Do you recycle at
home today?

Children who were enrolled as
salvage collectors, were known
as 'cogs' and were very keen.

The money was donated to the various
'Savings Drives' such as 'Buy a **Lancaster**'
(a type of bomber aircraft) or 'build a
Destroyer' (a warship). Slogans appeared
in schools like, 'Just an envelope will make a
cartridge wad' and 'Put your waste paper on active
service'. 'Scrap Metal Drives' were very popular. Metal could
be melted down and made into tanks or guns. At times
children could be seen walking into school carrying pots,
pans, bedsteads and tin baths!

Some schools also had salvage dustbins for pigswill,
bones, bottles and jars and rags. The slogan next to the bin
might have said: 'Bones = nitro-glycerine, glue, animal
foodstuffs, fertilizers'.

P.H.D.
BONES

Standards and attendance

It is not surprising that with all the movement of pupils, the Blitz, huge turnover of teaching staff, part-time schooling, make-shift accommodation and lack of equipment, educational standards dropped during 1939-45.

This was not true for the whole of the country, for some parts of Britain were hardly affected by the war, but in the industrial centres and big cities the quality of children's education suffered.

Another reason that led to children not progressing so well at school was **absenteeism**, meaning that children didn't turn up at school. The Blitz severely damaged the transport system and some days it was impossible for pupils to get to school.

Children assist two soldiers to salvage sweets from a bombed-out sweet shop.

Rationing and food shortages caused problems for families. If there was a rumour that a local shop was going to get a certain food in, older children were often asked to queue outside the shop by their mothers, who might have younger children to look after. This might take most of the day, so school was missed.

There was a huge demand for war work and wages for most workers went up during the war. Many women got jobs in factories even if they had young children. Older children were sometimes expected to stay at home to look after young brothers or sisters.

With coal in short supply, these children scramble for firewood after an air-raid.

When fathers on active service came home on leave, children took time off to see them. These were great moments in a child's life and families would make the most of those precious few days.

Some children took advantage of the chaos and confusion and truanted, often hiding in bomb-damaged houses and buildings.

Think about
The level of crime for young people increased during the war by about 33%. Why do you think this was?

Extra-curricular activities

There was plenty going on outside school for children to 'do their bit' and help the war effort. In 1941, the Air Training Corps (ATC) was started to help train young boys who wanted to join the Royal Air Force. The Sea Cadet Corps and the Army Cadet Force followed this in 1942. Any boy over 14 could join these groups and learn map reading, navigation, sailing, **Morse code** and aircraft identification. Some boys in the ATC went gliding.

The Girls Training Corps and the Women's Junior Air Corps were formed for girls and they learned signalling drills, First Aid and also provided important back-up for the Civil Defence and the Women's Voluntary Service (WVS). These organizations often had uniforms, which made them exciting and made children feel they were doing something worthwhile.

Think about
Which organization would you have joined to 'do your bit'?

The Enfield Boys Brigade mend toys for these young children from a nursery school.

This class of school boys learn to identify enemy aircraft during 1941.

The Boy Scouts and Girl Guides did very well during the war and had one million members. They did excellent work for the war effort by helping many organizations, especially hospitals. Boys checked fire buckets and stirrup pumps and girls assisted in the kitchens, preparing suppers, washing up and even cooking for the nurses. Scouts and Guides were always active in the salvage campaigns and at the forefront of the collection weeks for waste paper, silver, scrap iron, jam jars and cotton reels.

You did not have to be in an organization to help. Two 13-year-old twin brothers volunteered as messengers for the Fire Brigade during the V-1 and V-2 (both German missile names, 'V' stood for *Vergeltung* – 'revenge') Blitz in 1944. One of them helped drag a girl from a destroyed building and was congratulated by a Chief Superintendent of Police. The boy had saved the chief's daughter!

INSIDE STORY:

'I belonged to the Cadet corps. I enjoyed the Signals section and liked the Morse codes. We also did drill and weapon training, tactics and map reading. When I joined the army in 1942, I joined the Signals section.'

In the country

One very popular way for children to help with the war effort was through 'Harvest Camps', which took place during the summer holidays. The camps were a cheap and useful way of having a holiday even though they involved a lot of hard work! Thousands of children each summer set to work helping farmers to bring in the harvest, pick fruit and vegetables and help with general jobs around the farm. Some children learned to milk cows and goats, make butter, feed chickens and collect the eggs.

Despite the Women's Land Army (women volunteering to work in agriculture), there was still a shortage of workers in the countryside so the camps did make a big difference. The peak year was in 1943 when nearly 70,000 children were working on the farms. The poster campaign 'Lend a hand on the land – at a farming holiday camp' seemed to work.

With long days in the open air and sunshine, many children loved 'doing their bit' on the farm.

INSIDE STORY:

'Come September us children were needed to help with the harvest. We stacked the sheaves in the fields. Six sheaves made a 'stook' with a hole in the middle. We used to run through it and then we got told off for knocking them over!'

These evacuated girls from Gants Hill, London, worked two hours a day helping the farmer collect his potato crop.

'Harvest Camps' were a great opportunity for evacuees to be able to meet up with their mothers for a couple of weeks. Evenings were very pleasurable – after a hard day's work there were songs around a log fire and dances were held at the weekend. College students were keen to sign up in the holidays because they were paid between 24s 6d (£1.22 ½p) and 30s (£1.50) a week as well as board and lodging.

Children could also make a little money by picking rosehips. These were made into rosehip syrup, high in Vitamin C, at a time when oranges were very rare and were paid 2d (1p) for a lb of rosehips!

Think about
Why do you think 'Harvest Camps' were so popular?

On the front line!

Although the main Blitz lasted between September 1940 and May 1941 when all the major cities in Britain were bombed, the *Luftwaffe* (the German Air Force) still attacked towns, cities and ports in southern and eastern England. This placed a strain on the population and schools had to continue to be **vigilant** against these attacks.

Sometimes groups of German planes would fly to a city, 'strafe' (machine gun) the streets, drop their bombs and fly swiftly back to their bases in France. These were called 'hit and run' raids. Only one plane might be involved and it was often impossible to warn of the attack. Schools were very vulnerable, because large numbers of people were together in a small area.

Children were constantly drilled and taught to shelter under their desks in a 'hit and run' raid.

The funeral at Hither Green cemetery, south London of the children and teachers killed in the Sandhurst Road air-raid, on 27th January 1943.

On 20th January 1943, a German plane flew above Catford in southeast London and began strafing the streets. People dived for cover. As the plane approached Sandhurst Road School it dropped a bomb. There was a large explosion and the school was engulfed in flames. In the chaos, children – many of them hurt – ran screaming out of the school. Thirty-eight children between the ages of 5 and 15 were killed, as were six members of staff.

In the summer of 1944, the V-1 and V-2 weapons rained down on London and the southeast. When the V-1 ran out of fuel, it crashed causing a massive explosion. One new teacher in London was showing her class some work on the board. When she turned round the children had all gone! In fact, they were hiding under their desks because they heard a V-1 engine cut out and were ready for the explosion.

Think about
When the V-2 rockets started falling, the government at first denied they were rockets saying that gas mains had exploded. Why do you think they said this?

The cost of the war

When World War II ended in the summer of 1945, plans to improve education were already underway. A law passed in 1944 had made secondary education free for everyone and nationwide lectures called 'the schools of the future' were held.

What happened to the generation of wartime school children? What of the disruption that affected their education for nearly six years? Clearly, they had seriously suffered as a result of the shortages and upheavals. The quality of teaching varied enormously because replacement teachers were often inexperienced or were well past the age of retirement.

The problems of the Blitz and evacuation were damaging because they meant children often became part-time students. School Inspectors agreed that standards in reading, writing and arithmetic fell. Performances in other subjects like history and geography also declined. This meant that many children missed out on a good education.

Evacuation was a massive interruption in the education of millions of children.

Think about
How do you think you would feel if your family was separated because of a war?

On the other hand, it is true that some of the experiences of the war generation were positive. They had to be more independent and resourceful and learn to stand up for themselves. Those who were evacuated often had to look out for their younger siblings and became less selfish. Of course, many learnt a lot about the countryside and how farming worked. Many of the memories are undoubtedly happy.

The war had made people take notice of children. The government saw to it that they were fed better and school dinners, cod liver oil, orange juice, milk and vitamins became more important. As a result children's health improved. After the war, children and their education became a priority for the British government.

The end of war brought many fathers home to their wives and children.

INSIDE STORY:

'*Nothing was ever stable ... The main thing I missed out on was my education ... a missed education is something you can never replace. I felt I had to grow up far too quickly.*'

Timeline

- **30 August 1939** — Evacuation of 1.5 million children from all the major towns and cities.

- **3 September 1939** — World War II begins.

- **4 September 1939** — National Service (Armed Forces) Act. The call-up for all men between the ages of 18 and 41 begins (including 20,000 male teachers).

- **15 September 1939** — 'Dig for Victory' campaign begins.

- **January 1940** — In the absence of falling bombs, thousands of children return home to the cities.

- **Summer 1940** — Second evacuation of children begins because of German military successes in France and the Low Countries.

- **September 1940** — The Blitz begins. Many schools destroyed or damaged.

- **Summer 1942** — 'Lend a hand on the land' campaign begins and 'Harvest Camps' follow.

- **29 September 1942** — Petworth Boy's School, Petworth, West Sussex, bombed. Twenty-eight children and two members of staff are killed.

- **20 January 1943** — Sandhurst Road School, south London is bombed. Thirty-eight children and six members of staff are killed.

- **8 May 1945** — VE Day (Victory in Europe Day) celebrates the end of war in Europe.

Glossary

Absenteeism Frequent absence from school (or work).

Allied The countries that joined together to fight the war against Nazi Germany.

Battle of the Atlantic The battle to protect Britain's sea lanes from the threat of German U-boats.

Billeted When evacuees or soldiers are lodged in private houses.

Blast wall Walls built to protect buildings and people from bomb explosions.

Blitz The bombing of British towns and cities by German aircraft in World War II.

Civilian An ordinary person that is not in the armed forces.

Curriculum The subjects that pupils study at school.

D-Day The date when Britain, Canada and the USA invaded northwest Europe, 6 June 1944.

Destroyer Light, fast warships that protect other ships.

Evacuation To send people away from a place of danger in order to protect them.

Lancaster The Royal Air Force's most successful heavy bomber aircraft.

Manhole A covered opening through which a person could exit an underground shelter.

Morse code A code where letters are represented by long or short sounds or light flashes.

Patriotic When a person is loyal to his or her own country.

Reception areas The places where evacuated children were received and given shelter.

Salvage The saving and re-use of waste paper or scrap metal.

Shift system A set period of time for study or work.

Slit trenches A simple trench dug for pupils to shelter from air-raids.

Splints A length of firm material tied to an injured part of the body to stop movement.

Stirrup pump A portable water pump with a stirrup-shaped foot rest, used for putting out small fires.

Vigilant Constantly on the look-out for possible danger.

Further information

Books to read

In the War: Food and Rationing by Peter Hicks (Wayland, 2008)

In the War: The Blitz by Simon Adams (Wayland, 2008)

In the War: Evacuation by Simon Adams (Wayland, 2008)

Britain at War : Rationing by Martin Parsons (Wayland, 1999)

William at War by Richmal Crompton (Macmillan Children's Books, 1995)

Websites

http://www.bbc.co.uk/history/worldwars/wwtwo
BBC history site on WWII.

http://www.bbc.co.uk/history/ww2children/
Site on what life was like for children in World War II.

Note to parents and teachers: Every effort has been made by the publishers to ensure that these websites are suitable for children. However, because of the nature of the Internet, it is impossible to guarantee that the contents of these sites will not be altered. We strongly advise that Internet access is supervised by a responsible adult.

Index

Numbers in **bold** refer to pictures and captions.